Rags to Rags

Rags to Rags

essays on being a poor kid in wealthy spaces

Ellie Guzman

atmosphere press

Dedicated to Fidel Marquez.

Special thanks to...

Abbie Kopf
Alexander Medina
Alicia Fonseca
Amy Crisp
Andrei Draganescu
Bryan Kim
Cara O'Driscoll
Catherine John
Chase McCann
Christine King
Chuck Miller
Clare Mulligan
Daan Spijer
David Dayhoff
Desi Dmt
Ernio Hernandez
Guy Vincent
The Guzmans
Holly Veale
J.H. Gutbloom
Jack Herlocker
Jaimee Halstead

James Reeves
Jeanne Hoppe
Jo Simons
John Horner
John Mills
Joan Westenberg
Julia Garcia de Leon
Julie Coats
Kalpita Kothary
Katie Robleski
Kenneth Muiruri
Laura Barraclough
Linda Mondragon
Maria R. Randazzo
Mary Beck
Mikaela Ortstein
Paul Williams
Shakeel Soogun
Sherry Caris
Tori Scallan
Yael Acre

Introduction

I grew up living paycheck to paycheck; as a child I didn't think much of it, but once I hit my tween years I slowly figured out that not everyone hides from the landlord when rent is due. Even though I grew up without money, I always find myself surrounded by those who have it.

Throughout my entire life, I've accidentally infiltrated wealthy spaces, regardless of my own personal poverty. I don't do it on purpose; my life just happens to work out that way. As a child, I stumbled into commercial acting and was surrounded by an industry that burns money, and as a college student I ended up smack dab in the middle of one of the richest student populations in the United States. Now, as an adult, I'm navigating a career in the entertainment industry surrounded by people who have stuff like lake houses and investments while I'm still trying to figure out exactly what a "Fico" is.

Observing wealth from close range but being unable to participate in it has been, in a word, weird, but more than anything it's been amusing. Sometimes I've gotten envious, and I've pitied myself and my torn up sneakers, but never for long. Growing up broke has made me who I am, and I no longer feel like a fish out of water in fancy surroundings. I'm more like a fish who's going to sneakily grab some hors d'oeuvres for the road, cram them into my outlet mall purse, and quickly brush off any crumbs on the side of my $12 dress. But who even cares? After all, what's the difference between my cheap dress and designer wear? People can embellish them and call them different things, but at the end of the day they're both rags.

They'd also both look good on me, but that's beside the point.

This is a collection of essays about being the poorest kid in the room. Some are funny, some are angry, most are both. I hope you enjoy it.

-Ellie

Broke Living Tip #1:

If you crack an egg in your instant ramen, you can
pretend you're at a restaurant and not at home watching
YouTube videos of people falling down.

Am I Poor?

I never 100% understood what "poor" meant. It was kind of this all or nothing concept: a person either has a comfortable life with food and a home, or they're poor. I had food and a home, so I didn't feel poor. To me, poverty was little kids in foreign countries with their bones poking out and people in the street begging for money. When my family spoke of poverty, they'd refer back to their home in El Salvador, and the war and starvation that they left behind. Compared to that, I felt like a millionaire.

But as I grew older, things started to nag at me. I remember one day when it was raining heavily and my mother and I were waiting at a bus stop. I was about eight, watching the cars whiz by, and I silently wondered why we couldn't just jump in a car, drive it home, and leave it on the street for another family in need to take it wherever they wanted.

Wait, did eight-year-old me invent ZipCar?

Shit.

That was the first time I noticed that we didn't have things that other people seemed to have, and it was like a switch had been turned on. I noticed that other kids had different clothes they wore each week, not the same five outfits on rotation like me. They also had different pairs of shoes, instead of just one old pair of tattered Sketchers. Their moms stayed home a lot of the time, while my own mom cleaned houses and was always trying to sell random shit from catalogues wherever we went.

I kept my suspicions to myself, but it kept nagging at me. I'd stare at my dolls from the 99 Cents Store, quietly noting that they had mismatched stickers for eyes instead of painted on features like the ones from Toys R Us. I didn't particularly care; dolls were dolls, after all. I did, however, hate the feeling that something was being hidden from me.

I knew I couldn't go to my parents with these suspicions, so I did what any nerdy kid would do: I asked a teacher.

"Mr. Marquez, am I poor?"

He stared at me. He was my old kindergarten teacher, the first person who had noticed my intellectual curiosity and had taken me under his wing. I spent a lot of time with him due to the fact that my elementary school operated in four separate tracks back then, and usually my track was out of session while his was still active. The school knew that the track system could negatively impact families without a nanny or stay-at-home parent, so they offered extracurricular activities during breaks. One of these activities was acting as a teacher's aide, and so I was Mr. Marquez's aide from ages seven to ten. Usually aides bounced from class to class, but he asked that I work with him every session, and I didn't mind because I loved spending my days with him and the kindergarteners. At the time I thought I was a bigshot responsible cool grownup kid. Looking back now I know he wanted to keep me off the streets, keep me intellectually stimulated, teach me the value of responsibility, and maybe turn me into a mini teacher. It was also free childcare, so my parents had me do the program every single break for several years.

As soon as I asked him if I was poor, I felt the embarrassment creeping up over my face and looked anywhere but at him. He turned to me, his brows raised while pouring soy sauce over his noodles. We were having lunch between the morning and afternoon class of kindergarteners, and he had brought me some noodles as well. He'd been teaching me to eat with chopsticks, and I was picking at my food, slowly eating one noodle at a time.

I remember he gave it to me straight. He told me that yes, I lived in an economically disadvantaged area, and yes, my immigrant parents didn't have much money. But he also told me I was smart, and that someday I'd go to college and break out of the cycle of poverty. I told him my aunt said college was for rich kids, and he asked me what my parents said. I told him they thought I was smart enough for a scholarship.

"Then listen to them," he said.

I can vividly remember him scooping a noodle into his mouth as he leaned back in his chair and said with a smile, "If you try, you will. Eat your noodles."

I ate my noodles and that was that. That's why I loved spending time with him; he never talked down to me. My parents wanted to protect me so badly that they'd always tell me, "Don't worry baby, we're always here to take care of you," while Mr. Marquez was the one who spoke to me like I was a person with my own thoughts and concerns, even when I was a kid. That's why he was a great educator.

Mr. Marquez died when I was 12. I remember my parents telling me after I'd finished a dance recital at my new school. They said they hadn't told me until a couple weeks after he passed because they didn't want me to be distracted for the show. I locked myself in the bathroom and slumped against it, hyperventilating. He was dead. I'd never talk to him again.

My mother took me to his memorial a few days later. She had her own car by then, and I sat in it while she pulled over to buy flowers. I listened to oldies radio and chewed on my inner cheeks. *"Only you can make this world seem right, only you can make the darkness bright."*

I turned off the radio and pulled my sweater over my face.

We arrived at his house. It was a sizable property in a nice Los Angeles neighborhood, tastefully decorated and full of people who loved him. I realized Mr. Marquez had money, enough money to not teach in such a poor area of LA. I saw a wall of his house covered from ceiling to floor in drawings made by kids he taught. His friends had made a Scrabble board to memorialize him, which included the words teacher, friend, and love. He taught because he loved it, and in turn he was loved.

I met his brothers, who said they'd heard of me. They told me things about Mr. Marquez that I didn't know, like his love for *Will and Grace*. They all said "Just Jack!" in unison as I giggled through my tears. The memorial was bittersweet and difficult, but I'm so grateful to have gone.

Mr. Marquez taught me how to take ownership over my life. He knew enough about me and my family to tell me honestly that yes, I was poor, but I had the power to change my life. He challenged me and taught me responsibility, not just by having me help out in his classroom but by talking about the world and its hardships with me. He took it upon himself when he didn't have to, and he taught me from an early age that the world isn't rosy but that I was smart enough to equip myself to accomplish anything. He changed my life.

I wish he was here, and I wish I could thank him. I wish he could see that it's legal for him to marry in California now. I wish he could see that my dreams came true. I wish he could see the *Will & Grace* revival because it turned out better than people thought it would.

About a year after Mr. Marquez died, I was talking with my dad about what high school I would attend. We were sitting at the kitchen table in our little one bedroom apartment one Saturday, the school brochures sorted into piles next to a bowl of fruit. I made a remark about wishing Mr. Marquez was there to help out, and we began reminiscing about him. I smiled to myself, remembering those noodles.

"Yeah, back when I was eight and I first realized we're kinda poor, Mr. Marquez really set me straight on-"

"I'm sorry. You said we're poor?"

My dad looked at me, and my stomach dropped. *Oh*, I thought, *so it's time to finally have this conversation.*

Unfortunately, I was 13, and I had recently become a massive asshole. Call it a breakdown after being faced with the reality of my loved ones' mortality or just being a freshly minted teen, but I was on a roll with being shitty.

So I said, "Yeah, duh. We're poor." My dad simply stared, so I kept talking, years of repressed thoughts rushing out of my mouth. "I mean, look at this place. It's a one bedroom and we're four people. That's not normal. And look at the neighborhood. It's..." He maintained eye contact, as if daring me to say "shitty" or "sketchy". I sighed and just kept going through the brochures. My dad dove into them as well.

"This one looks nice," he said, passing it to me and ignoring everything I'd said.

The next weekend, he asked me to come with him to Tijuana because he needed to run an errand. I naively agreed, not realizing the errand was shaming me for my sins.

My father took me on a walk in front of nearly every single child selling Chiclets in Tijuana. The kids were thin, had clothes with holes in them, and were covered in dust and dirt from being near the road the whole day. Many of them were barefoot and most of them appeared to be alone. More than anything, the kids looked incredibly young. Their eyes were wide and innocent, but they were also narrowed and darted in all directions as they kept an eye out for customers and passing cars. We spent what felt like an eternity soaking in the image of these tiny kids, no older than ten years old, trying to sell little gum packets for 25 cents apiece. My dad turned and looked me dead in the eyes.

"*That* is being poor," he whispered in English, subtly pointing at the kids. I hung my head and tried not to throw myself into oncoming traffic.

"Did we really drive five hours to come look at this?" I asked. He nodded.

I knew I should've never brought up our finances to my dad. I looked at the kids, just like the ones in the commercials, their bones poking out, begging for change. But I still heard Mr. Marquez's voice in my head reassuring me that I wasn't being a brat for noticing my own family's situation.

We were not selling-Chiclets-in-Tijuana poor, but that didn't negate the reality of our situation. We still lived paycheck to paycheck, and my parents had loans all over the place. There was never a time that we weren't in debt. Our apartment was small and cramped. We had an eight hour wait at the clinic whenever we were feeling sick. My mom kept trying to sell cheap makeup and crystal bowls from catalogues. We never starved or had nowhere to go, but my family's financial issues came with their own painful struggles. Money greatly impacted my childhood and the way I saw the world, and I wanted nothing more than to talk to my parents about it.

But after the Tijuana trip, I never brought up feeling poor ever again.

Broke Living Tip #2:

You can save quite a bit of money on gas by taking the doors off the car to make it less heavy, never shifting off neutral and seeing where gravity takes you, or just staying in bed all day instead.

Child Actress

I loved attention as a kid. I lived for it. I think that because my parents didn't have much money, they overcompensated by giving me insane amounts of attention. When he wasn't working, my father videotaped nearly every single thing I did, from walking around at the park to dancing like a maniac in cow-printed pajamas. My parents spoiled me with attention, taking hundreds of pictures with disposable cameras and agreeing to all of my crazy whims. It was silly fun, but like all silly fun things (I'm looking at you, day-drinking) there came a point where it blew up in my face.

One day when I was five years old, I was doing my favorite activity: watching TV while stuffing my face. A commercial for a local business came up. This place was like a Costco-meets-Best-Buy for Latin American people in the US, and my family had purchased nearly all our furniture there because they did business in Spanish and offered layaway. It was like Candyland for them.

The commercial advertised a children's talent show, asking viewers to send in a photo of their child being silly to secure a spot in the contest. I immediately turned to my mom, who was then pregnant with my younger sister, and begged her to turn in my photo. She sighed and agreed, mostly to shut me up.

I was accepted into the first round of the talent show, and my parents and I made our way to the store a few weeks later. I was one of the youngest kids there, and we didn't know I'd need to perform so we had nothing prepared. I went up to the stage and the host asked about my special skill. I shrugged. He asked if I had hobbies.

"What's that?" I asked, never having heard of a "hobby".

"Something you love," the host replied.

"I love my mom and dad!" I shouted, throwing my arms up, and the crowd just about shit themselves from how cute it was. I made it to the next round, and then the next, and then the next.

Suddenly my mom and I were traveling around LA in buses, going from office to office as I continued to advance in the contest. I made it to the final four and that's when it got real; we'd be filming segments for Univision at Universal Studios Hollywood, and the audience would call in to vote for the winner, who would then get a spot in a Saturday children's show.

We went to Universal Studios and had a blast. One of the weathermen from Univision joined us, and the contestants were filmed individually trying out the different attractions, doing short reports in Spanish, and just being cute kids in general. Each of the four contestants received a small, five minute moment on TV; mine consisted of reporting from the old *Wild Wild West* attraction. My mom gently prepared me for the possibility of not winning since all the other kids were older and more polished, but I didn't really understand what she was saying because I was having so much fun. I didn't even realize the contest was still happening.

A few days after the segment aired, my mom received a phone call telling her that no, I hadn't won, because a five-year-old spearheading a children's show is balls to the wall insane, but that the studio had arranged meetings for me with local talent agents. If I could go back in time to this moment, I'd scoop up my 1998 self and swiftly fling her out the window because that'd be less painful than the coming years.

I signed with an agency that loved me (and my bowl cut), and they called me in for a couple of auditions. I began steadily booking commercials and voiceover work, and things snowballed. The first gigs brought money, the money brought headshots, the headshots brought more auditions, more gigs, more money. A year after the contest, I was suddenly a child actress.

It became routine for my mother to pick me up from school an hour early to take me to auditions in Hollywood, Burbank, and Santa Monica. My dad was still working two jobs, so she and my sister and I made our way all over Los Angeles on the bus, folding and unfolding the baby stroller over and over again. It was worth it: money started pouring in, and I ended up receiving 75% of it by check (10% went to my agent and the last 15% to my Coogan Account which mandates that child actors have at least 15% in a trust). My parents cashed that 75% and used it to cover things like my clothes and my prized Game Boy, as well as some of the expenses that came with the birth of my sister. I didn't mind it, and I never felt like my parents unjustly took any money. It was simply a small bonus income and they made use of it, also making sure I enjoyed my own things like video games.

I was just working commercials so I wasn't making insane amounts of money, but each $600 check made a big difference for my family. We were still considerably poor, but my steady work at least let us begin to break even. Because of that money, I was able to pay dues for a Screen Actors Guild membership. When I was eight, three years into my acting career, my mother was able to get a car for herself. Slowly, we were on our way up. I was in that sweet spot where I was working steadily, but I still had enough time for school and friends. I did a lot of commercials, but I wasn't one of those zonked out kids. Things were working out perfectly.

But, tragically, nothing gold can stay. At around age ten I hit puberty, and suddenly I wasn't as cute, I had C-cup boobs and a unibrow, and I was engulfed with tween angst. I continued going to auditions and still booked some gigs, but that's when I heard it start.

"What size is she again?"

"Hun, can you please fill out your height and weight on the form?"

"She's a little too busty, I think."

"Have you thought about plucking your brows? I know a great lady on Melrose."

"Do you exercise at all?"

I noticed that when my mother would fill out forms, she'd write that I was 100 pounds instead of 130. When I'd get fitted for wardrobe before filming, the stylists would dig around in frustration looking for something that would fit me since my mother would often lie about my size on forms. Girls started getting taller and thinner than me, and my short round frame that was handed down from generation to generation of my Central American family betrayed me. Everyone was white, everyone was statuesque, and I looked like a brown Weeble Wobble standing next to a bunch of Barbies.

I knew my mother felt similarly when she'd sit in the waiting room with all the other stage moms, what with their jewelry and perfect hair. She started going to Ross

Dress for Less and Marshall's, paying $20 for purses that were originally $80 and clutching them to her chest while we sat at auditions as a sort of armor. She'd find unflattering frilly shirts and shove them at me, ranting about what brand they were. Then I'd go into the dressing room and cry by myself when they didn't fit, and I began to feed my low self-esteem with angsty music and shitty boys.

The whole fucking thing sucked ass.

I began hating going to auditions. My mother would be on edge, I'd be on edge, and I felt like there wasn't a way out. I'd go in and try my best, but I knew the storm that was coming when I got back into the car with my mother.

"How did it go? Did you smile? You didn't give them attitude did you?"

I knew my mother wanted me to do well and saw this as my ticket out of a life like hers. She wasn't necessarily a stage mom; it wasn't about fame, but about time and money. Here she was, year after year, taking her kid who had potential to auditions, but the kid had decided to be a real pain in the ass and was wasting everyone's time. In my mom's mind, I was just one good audition away from getting one of those Disney kid jobs that would pay for my college and beyond. In her eyes, I was a bratty potential star, but in the casting director's eyes, I was an emo Dora the Explorer lookalike who did not fit the roles they were casting.

She made me call my agent after every audition. At this point, I did not give a flying fuck about this man. Every audition he sent me to that involved me rubbing my tummy and going "mMMMMMM!!!" after biting into a hamburger made me want to jump off a bridge. But I'd call him because I knew that would stop my mother's tirade for a few minutes.

"Hi. Yeah, it went well. Cool. Mmmmhmm. Yeah."

My agent sensed that I was shriveling up and dying inside, and he had an idea. He wanted me to try theater classes. We were quick to let him know we could not afford that, but he said he knew of a class that was only $5 a month. I reluctantly showed up to the class, expecting a bunch of kids doing cartwheels and going, "Look at me!" Instead, I found a group of fellow young Latinos in similarly broke situations who wanted to act simply because they loved it. I sought refuge in this little family, and they ended up being my North Star as I got older and navigated the weirdness of first-generation life in LA.

As I transitioned from middle school to high school, I didn't go to as many auditions. I was focusing more on theater and my academics, and honestly I had completely checked out of anything involving being on screen. In a rare act of rebellion, I began tanking auditions on purpose. I'd pretend all was well until I went into the rooms, and then I'd give monotone readings or roll my eyes like an asshole. I got a weird thrill out of it, especially knowing that it was probably driving my mother and my agent insane. I knew I couldn't flat out quit because I'd get the whole "after everything we've sacrificed!" speech so I decided that I would make the industry quit on me instead.

By the time I was 14, I was going on maybe one audition a month. I was in high school, a straight A student, and as far as I was concerned that bullshit was behind me. I'd made peace with my financial situation, and even though my family still lived paycheck to paycheck, things didn't feel bad. I didn't feel like I should try harder at acting in order to earn us more money. Then my agent called with a secret audition about two blocks away from my school.

"It's for an untitled project, there's no script, you just go in and have fun. They want you to read a monologue of your choice."

I walked to the audition after school, not bothering to change my clothes or put on lipstick. I was called into the room and saw that there were five people at a table. They asked what monologue I'd chosen. I smiled, feeling pretty good about myself. I had chosen to perform the ramblings of Miss Teen USA 2007 contestant Caitlin Upton, Miss South Carolina. It made me laugh and that's all I cared about. So I started reciting it, and the people at the table started laughing, and the little demon inside of me that survived off of attention was reborn. They asked me if I'd be open to auditioning for Disney shows.

Wait, what?

The recent fame of Miley Cyrus, Selena Gomez, and Demi Lovato had sparked a movement in the industry to try to snatch up as many teenagers as possible and turn them into spunky dancing-singing-acting machines. The people at the audition worked for Disney casting and were quietly looking at local teens that already had representation. They had enjoyed my audition and wanted to send me to auditions for new Disney projects. I didn't know what to think; I wanted out of the industry and felt like I was about to be sucked back in. I knew that my mental health was best when I stayed away from it... but then I thought about the money.

"I'd love to!"

Suddenly I was back to auditioning all the time. My agent and mother were ecstatic, convinced that my previous disdain had been some kind of phase and that now

I was in it to win it. Unsurprisingly, all these auditions were filled to the brim with 5'10" 16-year-olds that looked 25 and my mental state just got worse, but all I could see was dollar signs. I didn't care for the fame or spectacle of it all as much as other people might have, but I did care very, very much about the money. I knew my family was getting by without me booking gigs anymore; I didn't feel any financial pressure from them, at least not as bad, but I knew that landing just one of these TV show gigs could change my life. We could move out of that cramped one bedroom apartment. I could have nice clothes that weren't all from Black Friday sales. I could save enough money for college and not have the pressure of a scholarship hanging over my head. I wanted it so bad I truly would've done anything for it. I finally understood my mom.

Thankfully, I didn't book any of those TV jobs. Would it have been nice to have more money? Yes. Would it have been nice to go through everything else? Nope. I can guarantee that I would have become one of those dead-eyed show kids who is wound so tight she snaps. It doesn't happen to every successful child actor, but it would have 100% happened to me. Shit, I had enough of a hard time keeping my sanity when I was just doing commercials for gas stations and cheese.

As soon as I found out that I got into college and that my financial aid package would make going to USC possible, I dropped my agent without a second thought. My mom kept the hope alive: she kept paying my SAG dues until 2013, but I was free, never to have to sit in those waiting rooms poring over my measurements and sucking in my stomach. My demons weren't gone, but the fuel feeding the fire was. As far as the money went, I figured I could brainstorm other ways to make a quick buck. After all, how hard could it be?

Broke Living Tip #3:

You can avoid paying an exorbitant amount of money at the doctor's office by just straight up dying.

The American Dream

There's a lot of misconceptions about college financial aid flying around. They're always on two opposite ends of the spectrum:

"If you're poor, you can't afford college. Just go work in a mill."

"If you're poor, college is free. You mooch off the rich donors."

Spoiler alert: neither of these is true.

By the time I applied to college, my family was better off than it was when I was a kid. My parents had both learned English. My father was working as a city bus driver, and my mother had established a reputation as an excellent nanny in the fancy parts of LA. We were still living paycheck to paycheck, but we weren't accruing more debt like we used to. Instead, my folks were focused on paying that debt off. It was pretty sweet, and college started to seem more attainable. My parents expected me to go to college and figure out the application and financial process myself, so I dove into the internet and tried to learn as much as I could.

I thought I was good enough as a student to get a scholarship, but that wasn't exactly true. School was easy to me because I enjoyed learning, but I didn't have any extra oomph to take me above and beyond. Sure, I had a high GPA, a 95th percentile SAT score, and extracurricular activities like volunteering and performing arts, but I was not exceptional. By the time I started looking into college as a 16-year-old, I was already too late for the merit based scholarships. I didn't start my own vaccine business out of my parents' garage when I was 12. I didn't go to Guatemala and help little kids learn to play chess or whatever the fuck when I was 14. I didn't go backpacking through Europe and experience humanity when I turned 16. My socioeconomic status made me an academic nonstarter from the moment I plopped out of my mom's butthole.

I was good enough to get in, sure, but I wasn't snazzy enough to get a scholarship anywhere. A lot of the kids applying to these scholarships had done scientific research as high schoolers, while my own high school barely had functioning microscopes. Some of them had even sat in on surgeries, because their dad's cousin's neighbor-in-law just happened to be Chief of Neurosurgery at St. Nepotist. I knew several people in college who received full scholarships and didn't even need them; their parents had more than enough money to pay their tuition without it being a burden.

I'm not saying that accomplished teens don't deserve scholarships. They do. Hey, if some 13-year-old does cool research instead of burning My Chemical Romance CDs for her friends, I salute her. But the kids who do revolutionary shit like that are often able to do it because they have a giant pile of money to help them do it in the first place. In short, academia thrives off a wealth funnel system and everything is terrible all the time always.

Take volunteering, for example. Volunteering is, at its core, a luxury; a volunteer needs free time, the financial freedom to do work without pay, a mode of transportation, a way to feed themselves if food is not offered, and access to information about different volunteer opportunities. Of course, the goal of volunteerism is to help others, but it can't be ignored that volunteer opportunities are often reserved for privileged people, especially when referring to high-school aged kids. I did some community service in high school a couple times a week, but it was nothing compared to kids who were able to do mission trips in the summer or help with hurricane repair in another state. Because privileged kids are able to do things like that, it stacks the deck against applicants who can't afford those experiences. Once the time comes to apply to college, the kids with the more unique experiences make more competitive applicants and end up receiving merit-based scholarships that they don't fully need in the first place.

Financial aid is a nuanced issue, and I was definitely misinformed about it while I was in high school. I had two college counselors at the time; the first straight up laughed and recommended I only apply to state schools. The second one thought I could just waltz into any school and never struggle with money at any point because I was a good student who did my homework. It sounds shitty, but the sad truth is that they'd both worked at a public high school for years and that was the reality that they knew.

Of course, just because it was their reality doesn't mean it was the truth.

I was given a university grant that was, to me, gigantic. However, it wasn't enough to cover everything, and my parents had to pay an amount that was both just low enough to be affordable for them, but just high enough to plunge them into debt again. I took out the maximum federal loan amounts each year to help out, but my parents still had to take out Parent PLUS loans for my last two years. Our loans combined are less than $50,000 with the majority of it on me, but for us, it might as well be a million dollars.

I tried moving back home during college to ease the burden, but my financial aid was adjusted so that the grant itself shrank but my family contribution did not, so my folks had to pay the same amount whether or not I was living in the school, which is ten different levels of fucked up. The game was rigged, so I ended up just moving back to school and tried not to think about it. Leaving school was never a conversation; my parents had faith (and still, I think, to this day have faith) that one day I'll make enough money to pay off my loans and theirs. Fingers crossed!

This is the part where someone opens their mouth to tell me that I did life wrong. A largely pervasive misconception about financial aid is that public school costs less and private school will bankrupt families. I've had dozens of people on the internet and in real life ask "Well why didn't you just go to public/state school?" with a smugness so suffocating you'd think they just solved world hunger.

I was accepted into public and private schools, and was faced with the following question: If a private school costs $60k and they're giving $50k in aid, and a public school costs $15k and they're giving $5k in aid, where should I go? The answer doesn't matter because they're both $10k. I decided I would much rather go to a prestigious private school that has more resources for me to succeed if the costs come out to the exact same. Not to mention that the tuition for private schools tends to fluctuate less, so it's easier to estimate costs more concretely. But it can be hard for people to comprehend this if they haven't actually seen the competing financial aid packages themselves; in my case, the family contribution was the same regardless of the school's own tuition and fees.

Another nugget of wisdom that some people on the internet have been kind of enough to offer is "Why didn't you go to community college first, or just not go to college at all?" I'll tell them why; I was not going to walk away from a college acceptance to a school like USC without a guarantee that I'd be able to get the same acceptance and financial aid package after years of community college. I was going to grab this opportunity the moment it was presented to me because it was once in a lifetime. And not going to college at all? Yeah, try being a child of immigrants who is also Latina and a woman and wants to be taken seriously and succeed professionally and financially without a college degree. Good luck with that.

Achieving the American Dream is not black and white. First generation kids, Latinx kids, any underrepresented kids don't just get a scholarship and walk into the college of their choice without any difficulty at all. Once they're there, the hustle doesn't end, and hard work by itself isn't enough. It's difficult, it's draining, and they'll have to crawl and scratch their way to belong. But they can do it, because I did.

Broke Living Tip #4:

You can save on makeup by never removing it. If you wait long enough, your mascara will naturally transition to eyeshadow.

Rich Kids

Culture shock. That's what everyone told me I was in for when I let them know I was going to the University of Southern California, also known as USC for short, or SC for anyone who loves beer pong and football. As soon as a warm "Congratulations!" slipped out of one of my high school teachers' mouths, the next words were "you are in for *such* a culture shock."

USC is well known in California for being a rich kid school. That's not necessarily true, but it's also not necessarily false. *The New York Times* states on their page "Economic diversity and student outcomes at the University of Southern California" that as of 2017, the median family income of a student was over $160,000. In addition, there was recently a scandal where some celebrities allegedly dropped thousands of dollars to get their Instagram influencer kids enrolled, so make of that what you will. On the flip side, their financial aid was so generous that I was able to go at all, so I'm not too bitter about whatever the rich kids were doing.

Back in 2011, I was blissfully naïve and influencers didn't exist so the sky was the limit. I told anyone who'd listen that I was going to USC. I wasn't afraid of culture shock; after all, I'd read the admissions brochure several times, so I was ready for anything that came my way.

Or so I thought. I'll never forget the day I moved into my dorm. I arrived with my parents early in the morning with a crazy smug/optimistic smile on my face. My roommate had already moved in and was off somewhere living it up, and my parents and I eyeballed her side of the room. My smile fell before I even registered what I was seeing.

Prada. Gucci. Oh my God, she'd even splurged on wall decals. Wall decals! Those are like twenty dollars at Target!

I saw my mother looking at my own desolate side of the room, some clothes on white hangers that didn't even have velvet on them and no body pillow in sight, just the grey bedspread. I said goodbye to my folks and figured I'd explore campus. Maybe I could find a cute poster to decorate my wall. I went to the bookstore and felt a sense of impending doom looking at the textbook prices, ranging from $75 to $300. Within two hours, I'd already found several flyers for work-study jobs and sent them all my resume.

Oh God, I realized, the panic slowly setting in, *I'm out of my league here, aren't I?*

By the time my roommate Haley came home on Sunday, I'd already gotten an IT work-study job and would be beginning there on Monday afternoon. I was a ball of nerves; first day of college and first day of having a non-acting related job all on the same day. Haley told me about herself while I listened, my scalp itching.

Oh, her mom works for the school. Oh, she lives in Malibu. Oh, she wants to go home on weekends because it's so much nicer and fancier there than it is in this weird part of LA. Oh, she has fancy friends that'll be coming over sometimes. Oh, she's had a laptop all through high school. Oh, she has a car. Oh, these are just some of her clothes because all of her clothes couldn't possibly fit in this tiny dorm.

Haley asked me about myself and I grinned, feeling like my face was stuck. I told her I was first generation, my family lived ten minutes from here in the non-snazzy area, and these were all the clothes I'd ever owned. I held no details back, stubbornly forcing myself through any embarrassment because I didn't want to keep my situation a secret. If I was going to be the poor kid, I was going to own it.

She leaned in dramatically and stage whispered, "Before my mom met my stepdad, she was a single mom and she lived around this neighborhood too." She nodded fervently and looked around even though we were the only two in the room. "I don't remember much of it but it was before we moved to Malibu." I smiled, making a quiet note of how she felt a need to whisper for that.

The other girls in my suite were nightmares compared to Haley. As the weeks passed I heard them regularly say things like "This neighborhood is so ghetto," and "Ugh if I don't go to Cabo I'm gonna kill myself," and "I'm rushing Delta Gamma Theta Beta Zeta Alpha Lambda backslash backslash I am rich dot com," and "Ugh, these cleaning ladies are just *ugh*," and I bit my tongue. They invited me out one night about a month into the school year and I accepted.

It was like *Mean Girls* meets *Les Miserables*. All I wanted was a goddamn loaf of bread.

The girls had one mission: get glam, look hot, go to frat parties, meet boys, be collegey. I said I didn't know what to wear, and my roommate began throwing clothes at me. She was a curvy girl too, and we were miraculously the same shoe size even though she was a foot taller than me. Before I knew it, I ended up on frat row in a $500 outfit and makeup done by my suitemates. It was like I was Cinderella, and I had five fairy godmothers who were also super drunk and fresh out of high school.

I attended the party and had my first courageous sips of jungle juice, feeling my worries melt away and thinking *Yo, this alcohol thing is dope.* A blonde guy made his way to me and I clutched at my drink, wondering what Justice Sonia Sotomayor would say if she saw me now.

"Hey, what's your name?" he shouted into my ear, leaning too close and smelling like the mall.

"Katie," I yelled, leaning into the *Mean Girls* fantasy.

"Where do you live?" he asked, the most non-creepy follow-up question to someone's name that you can think of after a ten-second conversation at a frat party.

"Fluor Tower!" I replied, shouting over the music.

"Oh! Lots of athletes live there! Are you an athlete?" he shouted back, and I began laughing maniacally. I supposed I could be an athlete, if having cripplingly low self-esteem and pretending not to is a sport.

I kept laughing and just slowly walked away from him, letting the booze enable my mania. I stumbled up to my roommate. "Oh my God, Haley, that guy thought I was an athlete-"

Haley shot me a wide eyed look and gestured toward a beer pong table. There, swaying, was one of our suitemates, Stephanie. She was being slowly led into a dark hallway by two guys holding her, one on each arm, propping her up as she swayed drunkenly with her head bobbing down.

Haley and I both shot forward at the same time.

"Hey, this is our friend, oh my God we thought we lost her!" Haley said, lunging and snatching Stephanie's arm. The guys still held on to her other arm.

"She wants to come with us!" they said, pulling her

back.

Haley kept smiling, still yanking on Stephanie. "No, we have to bring her home! She has a big test tomorrow!"

"Tomorrow's Saturday," the taller of the guys replied, still holding on to Stephanie.

The guys started laughing, this mocking, grating laugh that meant they thought they won and they were going to do awful things to this half-conscious girl.

I knew Haley didn't want to cause a scene or commit social suicide, and I also knew I didn't care about those things. The only thing I cared about was what Detective Olivia Benson would do.

"Umm, rape! RAPE! RAPE!" I began shouting, pointing at the guys with my third cup of jungle juice in my hand. "RAPE! RAPE!"

Haley turned to me, her jaw hanging open.

"RAAAAAPE!" I shouted over the loud music, barely audible, but pointing at the guys and trying to pull Stephanie with my other hand.

"You FUCKING BITCH!" the shorter guy shouted while the tall one pulled him way.

"BITCH!"

"RAPE!"

"YOU BITCH-"

"RRRAAAAAPE!"

"Let's get out of here," Haley said, pulling Stephanie out of the house as I followed suit.

We got out into the cold 2am air. We ran with Stephanie, pulling her behind us, until she stopped to projectile vomit over a bush. We quickly tied her hair up and I put my hand on her back because that's what people did in movies.

Haley was panting, out of breath from all the running, one hand on Stephanie's nest of hair as she turned to me.

"Did you just start shouting 'rape'?" she asked, looking at me with her mouth still open.

I nodded vigorously. "It's for Olivia Benson."

"Who?!"

"She's a detective. She and Stabler. She's SVU."

"I have no idea what you're talking about."

We carried Stephanie arm in arm back to the dorm and watched her puke once more. We texted the other girls that we had headed home, and they sent us happy face emoticons. We put Stephanie in bed on her side and left a plastic bag next to her. Haley and I finally made our way back to our room and I crawled into my bed with the outfit still on. We sat in silence for a moment.

"Do you want to watch *Bad Girls Club*?" Haley asked timidly, pointing at her laptop. I hugged my pillow and turned to face her.

"Hell yeah."

It didn't take long for me to realize that these girls were just as clueless as I was. They were just trying to figure themselves out, and live up to the expectations of college that they had in their own heads. The difference was that their expectations of college revolved more around tailgates and frat parties while mine revolved around being able to finally break the cycle of poverty for my family if I played my cards right because this was my only chance, no pressure or anything. At the end of the day we were all just wading through ponds of jungle juice and binging shows on our laptops, theirs a Macbook and mine a previously owned mini offbrand laptop that heated up to over 400 degrees whenever I went on YouTube and watched

"Breakdancer Kicks Baby."

Haley and I parted ways the next year, and I spent my time as a sophomore living with a girl who grew up so rich in China that I had to teach her step by step how to use a vacuum. I moved back home after that, but it wasn't cost effective, so I moved back to school for my senior year. That was when I finally hit the roommate jackpot.

My new roommate understood me in a way no one at USC really had; she was also a first generation Latina who had grown up like me. She was funny and kind, and she understood my references, and I understood hers, and we had a shorthand that I didn't experience with anyone else in school. One day when we were talking about our experiences, she mentioned that she'd never gone to a frat party. I was flabbergasted. I was done with the frat scene at that point, but begged her to go to a party that night, just for shits and giggles. Frat parties were a weird first-person look into the rich kid experience, plus there was free booze and stories to be made.

"No. We can't go to those!" she said, shaking her head fervently. I told her it would be funny but she kept shaking her head. I realized she was actually serious. "You know we go to this school, right? We can go to these parties!" I said excitedly. "There's nothing stopping us! Come on!"

She caved and came to the party with me, and it was everything I wanted her to experience. There were two open bars. There was a professional performing stage with an actual EDM DJ who blasted us with confetti and neon lights. There were hired security guards. It was weird and excessive and all the things we expected it to be. We scoffed at it, but we also threw our hands up and danced along with everyone else. For a little bit, we were part of the fantasy.

Broke Living Tip #5:

Buy clothes at thrift shops and places like Goodwill.
It's actually the hipster thing to do now, so really you're
just a trendsetter for wearing some dead guy's jean jacket.

You Better Work

Being alive is expensive. You need food, shelter, water, clothes, and every now and again a large triple dirty chai with soymilk. I was brokest in college, because I didn't want to ask my parents for money that they didn't have and my financial aid only covered tuition and housing. I still had to pay for my food, books, and any other expenses (look, dirty chais are delicious, okay?).

For the first couple years, having just one work-study job was fine. I worked in IT for about a year, and then I left for a job at a colorectal cancer study as a research intern. I kept this internship all throughout college because it was the best of both worlds: I learned about cancer research, and it was paid. I didn't need to make too much money; just enough to feed myself, pay for gas, buy textbooks, and occasionally invest in some weird underwear. As I got older, though, my expenses started piling up and I had to choose between taking out a credit card or getting another job, and I didn't want to burden future Ellie too much (thank you for that, past Ellie).

I began taking on odd jobs that wouldn't conflict with classes and my internship. I started driving for our school's private rideshare program. We had a selection of school-owned cars to drive, and I learned how to drive a Prius and a van without killing anyone. My nights consisted of driving around my classmates, sometimes up until 3 in the morning. I started delivering food as well, and in breaks between classes I'd pick up a delivery or two and make enough for my own dinner. The oddest job, though, was selling my body.

I'm not talking about sex work. That would be a better story, I think. Rather, I started volunteering myself for experiments, and it turns out that having a high body mass index meant I was high in demand for diabetes and weight loss studies. I was literally selling my actual physical body. At least I didn't have to shave.

There was a teeeeeny tiny voice in my head asking, "Am I really so broke that I need to drink some random substance for this experiment in order to be able to get by for the month?" Then there was another much louder voice in my head saying "That's $300, bitch!"

My favorite was a study where they were trying to figure out if overweight people's consumption of sugar led to them wanting more sugar. They would give me a sugary drink with a certain amount of fructose in it (randomly from 0% to over 50%), and then they'd shove me in an MRI machine for an hour and show me pictures of cake, chips, and other junk, and I would answer honestly about which I preferred. Then at the end of it they'd draw my blood, using the most phlebotomy-challenged nurse they could find. She'd stick me like 12 times until she could finally get some of my blood. Then I'd cheerily wave goodbye and go home to find myself craving cake for some reason.

Some of the experiments were psychological. In one of them I had to build a small boat out of Legos while a white guy yelled vague directions at me. It was probably the most metaphorically on-the-nose experience I had in college. In a couple others, I simply dropped by a lab and took surveys on the computer for an hour and left with a $10 Chipotle giftcard. That's a burrito and an Izze drink. I was living large.

I also scrounged for free food at school events. I went to lots of poetry readings to get free cookies and tea, and joined clubs for a slice of pizza. I accidentally joined a Jesus club once and sneakily crept away while holding a banana nut muffin in my cheek like a sacrilegious chipmunk. My lowest point was probably pretending to be a freshman so that I could steal an orientation sandwich. I acted like I was lost and everything, like "Oh? Is this the orientation table for sandwiches? I'm so lost! This school is so big!" It definitely would not have won me any acting awards.

If I ever ate lunch outside, I'd make sure I was close enough to a water fountain so I could take periodic sips and avoid buying a drink. It's a miracle I didn't get any diseases from that, not even parvo. I'd also wear workout clothes everywhere because they worked for class, for the gym, for sleeping, and even for my side jobs. I can't 100% confirm that I started the athleisure trend, but I at least had a significant hand in it. You're welcome, Lululemon.

Struggling for money all the time was not fun, but it made me learn a lot about myself. I know for a fact now that I am capable of hustling, and I feel proud of my determination and drive. I had friends in college who sometimes struggled too, but often they could lean on their parents to help alleviate some of the strain. I knew I would rather deliver a sandwich for some grad student than call my parents for cash. I knew my parents were so supportive that they'd take out yet another loan and not tell me, so I promised myself I would exhaust all possible options before going to them for help.

I grew up a lot thanks to my money problems in college, but it doesn't mean I want to do it again any time soon. I felt happy and fulfilled without money, but it was also constantly stressful. Even though I'm better off now, my old habits are still deeply ingrained in me. I hoard coupons. I'd still rather use a water fountain than pay $2 for a water bottle. I buy clothes that can be used for work and the gym and going out, because single-purpose clothes are ridiculous. It doesn't matter that I'm not in the same situation that I was in college. You can take the girl out of the broke, but you can't take the broke out of the girl.

Broke Living Tip #6:

When you can't afford to buy meat, poultry, or fish, just tell yourself you're a vegetarian. Now, it'll seem like a choice.

I Can't Afford to Find Myself

When I was in my junior year of college, my life fell apart very quickly. To make it short and sweet, my parents began living separately and filed for bankruptcy. My sister also had health issues and in the chaos of it all, I moved back home to try to help out. I was the good one, the eldest, the kid in the fancy college, and I tried desperately to hide that I was drowning emotionally, academically, physically, financially, you name it. All of the -ly's.

I wasn't the one going through the separation or the health issues, and I knew it wasn't about me. But it was happening to my loved ones and affecting me. My parents expected me to be perfect throughout the ordeal, and I ended up becoming the translator for my sister's health issues and the therapist for both of my parents while they couldn't stand each other. They'd call me at all hours of the day, even when I was in class, either to vent about each other or to ask me what side effects my sister's medications had. It made the environment I lived in suffocating and toxic, and I internalized the pressure to be quiet and perfect and support everyone else.

I didn't tell my family how I felt, so according to them I was doing great and handling everything beautifully. I was essentially living a double life with no one except my boyfriend knowing, and even he didn't realize how far off the deep end I'd gone. To be fair, I didn't really feel it until it was too late. Before I knew it, my grades were in the toilet and I was skipping class to drive to the beach and just stare at the waves for hours. I'd sleep over at friends' houses often just for an excuse to get mind-numbingly drunk. The only thing that stayed consistent was work, because now that my parents were bankrupt I knew I had to fend for myself more than ever. I could feel myself being sucked into depression, and it was terrifying. One of my friends had started seeing a therapist, and I saw how much it helped her, so I called my school's health center and asked what resources they offered. They told me that I could receive free help at the Occupational Therapy Center, and I scrambled for a same-day appointment.

The sessions worked. My therapist, Lily, was great, and together we filled out worksheets and calendars of how I could juggle the emotional clusterfuck I was in. She was great and made me feel really heard and validated. After a few weeks, I opened up more and told Lily I sometimes wished I could just hit pause on life, go hang out on a boat for like a year or two, and then unpause and come back, refreshed. I didn't want to end it all; I just wanted everyone to shut the fuck up and leave me alone for at least six months.

"Why don't you travel?" she asked, like it was the most obvious thing in the world. I raised my eyebrows. "Lots of students travel! You can take a semester off and go to Europe, or Asia, or South America!"

I looked around the room to stall and realized that, to Lily, I was just like most kids from USC who could just *poof* to another continent and not, you know, starve to death or live on the streets. I tried to remind her I was financially strapped but she still didn't understand.

"You could stay at a hostel! Tickets to Europe aren't too expensive this time of year; you can get a round trip for $600!"

She was so excited and sweet that I just nodded feebly

and muttered something about talking to my parents. I never did because I think if I asked them for money to travel while they were going through everything, they would've temporarily put aside their differences to place my head on a curb and happily hit it like a piñata.

A couple of years passed, and somehow, everything worked out. Things might actually be better than they were to begin with. My parents are back together and weirdly more stable and in love than ever (which honestly was a plot-twist but I'll take it). My sister's in excellent health. The financial issues are a day to day challenge but the bankruptcy is behind us. It was hard, but I'm also glad the experience taught me to check in with my own health and seek help when I need it. It also taught me to establish boundaries with my family, which was a long time coming.

Now that things have settled down, I would really like to travel. I think of Lily's advice often, and the idea of exploring the world has nagged at me for years. I just could never pull the trigger, not even after I graduated and things got better at home. It's not that I don't *want* to travel; I really frickin' want to. I get excited just doing a road trip up to San Francisco. I love seeing new places. I'm painfully aware that we only get one life to live, so I want to absorb as much of this planet Earth that I can while I'm still alive. I love going to hole-in-the-wall restaurants in new places. I absolutely adore exploring old buildings and sightseeing. I just about wet myself at the idea of biking through a quaint European town. I also know that that's not going to happen for me any time soon, but I'll keep it in my mind. Just, you know, let me save up for the next decade or so.

To this day, I still get people telling me to travel so that I can find myself. I heard it after graduation, when I was between jobs, and now that I'm working in a studio with people who travel all the time. I make more money now, but I'm years of saving away from just going to Japan for a week. I think about it often though, and I keep a list of places for "someday." But for now, the only way I'm going to find myself is if Google Maps tells me my soul is within walking distance.

Broke Living Tip #7:

Wine from the gas station tastes like wine from an elite
vineyard after six to seven glasses.

Window Shopping

Shopping with other people has always made me itchy. Shopping by myself can be a tolerable experience when I have the money for it (which comes about as frequently as Haley's Comet), but I think shopping with others is the ninth circle of hell. My options for shopping partners are family, my boyfriend, or friends – and to be honest it doesn't take much to want to headbutt my loved ones.

Shopping with family is dreadful because I end up spending eight hours following around my disorganized parents, and it becomes a fluorescent lit hostage situation. Time loses its meaning. Half of my childhood memories include burying myself into piles of puffy jackets at Costco while my parents scavenged for $15 sneakers.

Shopping with my significant other can either be boring or awkward if one of us is having an un-pretty day ("Does this look good on me? Why did you hesitate?"), but I'll admit it can also be a great time if he's actually buying me stuff. Once I was window shopping with my boyfriend, and I stared longingly at a $100 bottle of perfume. He had recently been approved for a credit card, so he guided me to the cashier and paid for it himself. That was actually my first real orgasm, but I'm not sure it was worth the seven months it took him to pay it off.

Shopping with friends is in my opinion the worst, because I think it's harder to get away with throwing a tantrum once I get sleepy. Plus, it's hard when you don't have as much money as they do. People have very different definitions of "broke." I love my friends, but to many of them, "broke" means that paying for a flight to Vegas tonight on impulse could be a bit of stretch, while "broke" for me means that I have $20 in my bank account after buying groceries. It's nothing against them; these are people I've met in college and working in the entertainment industry so obviously we all come from different backgrounds.

Shopping with female friends in particular is my ninth circle of hell because it presents a special problem to me; I wear plus size clothes while most of them do not. Of course, many affordable women's stores like Forever 21 and Target now have plus size sections, but this only happened recently in the post-Ashley Graham *Sports Illustrated* cover era. Back in college and high school, I would spend a lot of time in the accessories sections looking at handbags and pretending that was fine. My friends were more than happy to go to plus size stores with me, but any girl over a size 14 knows that plus size stores are ridiculously expensive. There were little miracles sometimes though; once I bought an Abercrombie & Fitch knit sweater that was on clearance and actually fit me. It was $15 and an Abercrombie XXXXL. Wow, they were so progressive for carrying those four Xs.

Since I couldn't fit into anything or even buy it if I did, I got really good at window shopping. There was a period in my life from ages 15-22 where window shopping was the shit. It was like I was in some magic fantasy land, where I could touch a fluffy jacket and think "mmm, that's nice," and then I'd just float away, onto the next blouse or tchotchke. I guess it was more handsy shopping than window shopping. I felt a lot of faux fur.

Now that being plus size is more mainstream (never mind that the majority of American women are over a size 12), I have more options, except that I really don't because there's the whole money thing. You see, shopping because I'm hyped up from watching *Legally Blonde* is fun, but shopping because I need a new pair of jeans since my old ones have an inner thigh hole from chub-rub is stressful.

I don't know if the dread for shopping will ever go away, even if I have money. Part of me thinks I'll be hovering in clearance sections forever, something deeply burned into my brain from childhood. Another part of me thinks I'll go bananas if I ever have enough money to burn, and I'll just buy dumb shit until I go bankrupt. Money is weird, and money is fickle, which is why window shopping is just fine for me.

Broke Living Tip #8:

If you fall asleep on the bus and wake up in another zip code, that's pretty much the same life experience as backpacking through Europe.

Love and Dating and Money

Dating is hard. You've got to spend time with someone, figure out if you like them or not, figure out if they like you or not, figure out if you like each other the same way, start fighting about stuff, get to know each other's deepest fears and weirdest quirks, and keep in mind that the whole thing might implode in your face. But dating while broke? That's a whole other thing.

Dating is, at its core, expensive. Everything that you do becomes an activity for two. You want to try a new restaurant? That's now two meals. You want to watch a new movie? That's two tickets. You want to go on a trip? Now it's a *couples'* trip.

Because I'm not a complete asshole, I believe in splitting up the cost of things. If my boyfriend pays for our dinner one day, I pay for dinner the next day. We often go splitsies too, which helps, but it still adds up. When you're in a relationship, you're much more likely to go outside, pay for activities, eat at restaurants, and spend more gas money than you would be if you weren't seeing anyone.

I'm a firm believer that you should be super open about your financial situation when you're in a relationship. Obviously, you don't want to tell someone your entire life story on the first date, but it should still come up around the time things become official. It's sad to see people try to keep up an illusion of having more money than they do while dating, going on expensive trips and to music festivals and so on, their partner not realizing that their significant other is taking out credit cards left and right. It's even worse when it's spouses hiding debts from each other, when they're supposed to be sharing a life together.

Talking about money can be ugly. Not everyone will understand a situation that isn't like what they grew up with, but you need to have tough conversations in relationships because otherwise what's the point? You should be open about when you're trying to save up or when you're in a tough spot, even if it makes you feel like a buzzkill.

It's also hard to find someone that is in the exact same financial situation that you're in, especially now that the dating pool is much wider thanks to technology and social media. Chances are, one partner will make more money than the other. Rather than assume that the one that makes more money will pay for everything, or that the one that makes less money will need to be "taken care of," there should be frank conversations happening about what financial expectations are. I know this can be awkward, but trust me, you do not want to be on the other side of this conversation. You don't want to be several years into a relationship or even married and realize that you have way different attitudes and priorities toward money. Sure, people with different economic attitudes can make it work, but not without serious compromise.

I'm passionate about this topic because I've seen what happens when a couple does not communicate well about money. My parents did the best they could, considering they came to the US with nothing and lived paycheck to paycheck for decades. The deal was that my mom would stay home taking care of the kids and trying to make money here and there with side hustles, and my dad would be the primary breadwinner, sometimes working two jobs at a time for years on end. Occasionally our situation would shift and my mom would take on a nannying job for a couple years, but the arrangement was more or less the same for long periods of time.

I spent my childhood witnessing my parents argue about money at least four times a week, if not more, until the day I left for college, and honestly even after that. I don't blame them for this; it makes sense. They were scraping by for a long time. They each had loans which had helped them get settled in this country, and they were doing blue collar work. They needed to provide for two kids, so of course things got tense and their priorities clashed. My dad wanted a house to leave behind for his kids, so he wanted to save; my mom wanted to make sure we had sturdy clothes and good food; and they both wanted us to have good experiences like going to theme parks every now and again and having new Halloween costumes every year. Both of them had their hearts in the right place, but they fought tirelessly about money. Sometimes they'd even take out loans without telling each other, and I'd listen to them fighting while feeling terribly guilty, knowing that if they didn't have my sister and me they'd be fine.

I promised myself that, even if my future relationships weren't perfect, they would know exactly where I stood about money. I knew we'd probably fight at some point, I mean all couples do, but never several times a week about money. I was *not* going to be taking out secret loans with a spouse and two kids at home who had no clue what was going on, and I sure as hell was going to be able to buy a $20 purse without having my husband grill me about where I got that money.

When I began dating my boyfriend B in high school, I had zero clue how long the relationship would last. All I knew was that I liked a cute boy and he liked me back. But the years passed, we both grew up, and now it's ten years later and our relationship is wonderful and healthy and fun. We casually talk about end-game stuff: what our kids will be like (insufferable smart-alecs, if you're wondering), where we'll live, what our vision for our life is. After we finished college and transitioned into actual adulthood, I figured we should talk about that old Guzman classic: money.

B and I are in super similar situations on the surface. We're both first generation children of immigrants. We both grew up living with one other sibling. We were raised within ten minutes of each other. We both went to college and took out some student loans. This is where the financial similarities end.

B doesn't have nearly the same amount of debt that I took on. B's family lives in a way, way nicer apartment than my family. B (get this) didn't witness, if I do the math right, over 1800 arguments about money growing up. B's family saved. So it's normal to him and now he saves. Once we talked about it, it was like something clicked and I understood things about our relationship dynamic that I had never thought about before. Money impacted my personality because it was a constant stressor since I was a kid, and I was shocked that another kid in a similar situation to mine didn't have the same terrifying anxiety that I did about cash. I realized that I assumed all first generation kids had the same experience that I did, which was incredibly self-centered. That also reinforced my view that it's important to have these money conversations early before taking major steps like moving in together.

Throughout our relationship, our budgets have shifted,

and we've had to adapt to each other's reality. First, we were high school students who borrowed $20 here and there from our parents, and we ordered the cheapest things on the menu at fast food places. Then we were college students with work-study jobs who made limited amounts of money, and we ordered the cheapest things at sit down restaurants. Then, after he transferred from community college to a four-year university, we were long-distance college students who saved our work-study earnings for gas when driving to see each other, and since he earned more than me at the time he'd pay for the bulk of things. Now we're Actual Adults living in the same place with full-time jobs, so we splurge a bit more on trips and fancier meals. Sometimes he's made more, sometimes I have, sometimes we've both made very little, and sometimes we've both been able to splurge. It's nice to know that we've managed to adapt to each other's financial ebbs and flows, and it's good practice for whatever comes at us in the future.

I understand that it's simplistic to think that conversations about money will get rid of money problems down the road. They most likely won't. We're in the millennial generation: we have crazy debt and housing sucks. We also don't know what will happen in the future. One of us could become unemployed, or be injured, or go through any other awful catastrophe that happens to people all the time. Regardless of what happens, I hope we never lose the ability to be open and honest with each other.

Broke Living Tip #9:

Walking is healthy and cheaper than driving or using a ride-sharing app. It can even be a fun workout when you're being chased down the street in broad daylight by some dude shouting about the apocalypse.

I'd Like to Speak to the Manager

It takes a lot to make me feel uncomfortable. I am not someone who's easily embarrassed or ashamed; for example, I'm writing the poverty diaries right now while wearing yesterday's pajamas and eating Cheetos Puffs. However, there's one thing that always, always makes me want to crawl into a hole and disappear forever. It's when I'm out at a restaurant or store or bikini wax emporium and whoever I'm with says the dreaded words:

"I'd like to speak to the manager."

This has only happened a few times, but every time I literally feel so uncomfortable that I either completely turn around and walk away or retreat into my phone and make myself as small as possible. I think it's because nine times out of ten, I feel a lot more like the employee being yelled at rather than the person doing the yelling.

It's not a rich/poor thing. My mom gets a kick out of emotionally manipulating cashiers until she gets the discount she wants, which, okay, might be a poor thing, but it's still not great. On the other side of the spectrum, I've also witnessed people I know who grew up with money pulling this stunt when their food is just a smidge cold, and I haaaaaate it.

I understand that this discomfort can make me a bit of a doormat. There have been times when I honestly really should have spoken to a manager. Like that one time when I asked for a latte with soymilk but they gave me normal milk and I spent my Wednesday glued to my toilet cursing the gods. Or that time when the girl at Forever 21 straight up forgot that I was waiting for a price check and simply left me standing there until I disappeared into ash like on *The Avengers*. Or that time at the bikini wax emporium when... you know, I'll save that one for myself.

The whole thing just feels so icky. I was raised to think that out there in the world, it was very "us versus them," with "us" being the cashiers and nannies and "them" being the guys in suits and ladies with expensive handbags. Thankfully I've mostly outgrown that narrow worldview, but moments that beat down on a person just doing their job still make my skin crawl. I think they affect me so powerfully because my entire family is part of the working class, and that's how I identify. The weird thing is, I'm now the lady with the handbag, ordering a venti raspberry mocha blended coffee with soymilk and two shots of espresso, stomping in my ankle booties on the way to the studio. Like, who the fuck is that?

It's a weird identity thing; I feel like "them", but I'm still very much a part of "us." Honestly it's all gibberish at this point. What I know deep down is my heart will always be with the working class. I don't care if I own a fucking spaceship, that will always be the case. I feel like if I lose that, I lose myself. So why would I want to make someone's life more difficult whenever I'm faced with an inconvenience, especially when I know what's it like to live paycheck to paycheck?

We never know what someone is going through, what their family situation is, how much money they have to eat today, and so on. Is it worth risking someone's job stability for a mild delay at the shoe store? Then again, do I honestly want to be a doormat? It's like this weird back and forth between anxiety and being able to sympathize financially, and honestly I'll just keep crawling into a hole whenever this happens and drinking my poisoned lattes because I would rather deal with an upset stomach than knowing I cost someone their job. Even if it was technically their fault. My latte will always pale in comparison to someone else's livelihood.

Now if you'll excuse me, I have to go to the bathroom.

Broke Living Tip #10:

Watching Beyoncé's "Single Ladies" video ten times a day and dancing along at home is the same as attending a concert.

Oh My God, Are You Bryan Cranston!?

Act One: Setup

I used to act in commercials as a kid, and this got me a nifty membership into the Screen Actors Guild. The years passed and I maintained my membership into my teenage years. When I was 19, I received a letter letting me know that I had been randomly chosen to be part of the group that nominates movies for the SAG Awards. Every SAG member can vote in the awards, but only a few can nominate the movies that other members will ultimately vote for. I'd be able to attend free screenings and exclusive Q&As with Fancy Famous People, and I was pretty stoked.

I said yes and attended some Q&As. Saw Eddie Redmayne, Matt Damon, and John Krasinski. Hotties. Appreciated good films. Snacked on snacks.

One event popped up in my email inviting me and a guest to an *Argo* screening in Hollywood at the Pickford Center (which is associated with the Academy of Motion Picture Arts and Sciences). It said to show up at six for a mixer with snacks and mingling and that at the end of the movie there would be a Q&A with possibly some of the cast and crew. They had me at snacks.

I invited my mom and she didn't want to go. Neither did my boyfriend. They both had things to do. I was a sophomore in college at this point so I too had things to do but the difference was that I did not want to do them. I invited my friend Robert, and he was also intrigued by the free food. We were off.

Act Two: Who The Hell Are You?

Some context: Robert and I were two 19 year old broke nerds. We wore jeans, sneakers, and casual tops to the event. We thought we were going to gorge ourselves on food and then watch a long movie, okay?! We didn't know! Oh God. We didn't know. We knew the building would be fancy because of the academy affiliation, so we wore *nice* casual tops. JC Penney and shit. I remember that my jeans were light blue, my sneakers were black and white, and my striped shirt was too short for me. I looked like a background *Family Guy* character.

Robert and I walked to the side entrance and smiled awkwardly at the bouncer. He cocked an eyebrow. I handed him my ID and gleefully announced that we were there for "the *Argo* thingy" because I was and still am insufferable. Robert and I stood there for a good five minutes while the bouncer triple checked his list and whispered to his friends Ms.FancyLadyWithAClipboard and Mr. TheOtherBouncer. Resigned, they realized that it was in fact me and my papers were legit (like in "Dirt Off Your Shoulder" by Jay-Z). They checked the contents of my bag (mints, Revlon ColorStay lipstick, and approximately 12 dollars), and we were finally allowed in.

Robert and I walked through a tunnel with a red carpet and stomped all over it like heathens in our Sketchers. We got in line and waited for the doors to open. This was when we began to notice that everyone was dressed to the nines and we smirked at each other. *Jeez, what a bunch of tryhards. It's just snacks and a movie.*

Act Three: It Was Not Just Snacks And A Movie

The doors opened and the line began moving. If I could go back to this moment, I'd grab Ellie and shove her into a TJ Maxx gown and tell her to network. I'd tell her to not freak out and be cool. I'd tell her to save me some coconut shrimp.

Tragically, the process of humiliation had already begun.

Robert and I entered through the doors and we marveled at the gorgeous room, all the food, and the beautiful people. The room was draped in red and gold, and there were long tables on either side laden with desserts and fancy food I'd never seen before (yes, I'd never seen hors d'oeuvres in the flesh before. I'm a poor kid from LA. Our version of a finger sandwich is when the lady from *Subway* loses one of her acrylics in your meatball sub). I looked ahead of me toward the bar, wondering if Robert and I could score some booze. As my eyes refocused, I realized I was looking Bryan Cranston right in the eyes and he was about four feet from me.

I can't capture with words what my brain was doing. All I can say is that everything moved in slow motion while Enya played in my head. I was not someone who was starstruck easily, but I hadn't had any chance to prepare for this. I had kept my cool around someone like Matt Damon because I *knew* I was going to see him, but this was an entirely different situation.

It was 2012; *Breaking Bad* was extremely popular and I watched it religiously. Also, I had grown up watching *Malcolm in the Middle*. This was absolutely nuts, and I was not emotionally prepared to suddenly be stuck in a room with this man.

I realized I had been staring at him for a good 30 seconds and immediately panicked. I looked to my right quickly and saw the most handsome man I had ever seen up to that point in my life (and beyond, let's be honest). He was broad-shouldered, tall, and so good-looking that I felt like I was staring at the sun. I was staring at one approximately 10 foot tall Ben Affleck *in the flesh*. I was always more of a Matt Damon girl, but the moment I saw Ben Affleck I knew that I was forever changed. I wanted to ride that man like a horse into the sunset. Too much? No, buddy, not enough.

I will forever be proud of the fact that I didn't flat-out faint at that point.

I realized I'd lost Robert and began looking for him. I searched for him in a daze and found him standing wide-eyed at one of the buffet tables, stuffing macarons in his mouth with glazed-over eyes.

"Robert?"

"E... Ellie... there's..." Robert raised his finger like E.T. and pointed toward the distance. I glanced over my shoulder and realized he was pointing at a very orange George Clooney.

I looked back at Robert, who was trying to make himself look as small as possible.

"I've never even seen a famous person on the street," he whispered, all but curling into a ball, "and now they're here..."

I sighed and looked down at my blue jeans and sneakers.

"Yeah," I muttered, looking back up and seeing all the Fancy People mingling with the other Fancy People, "I fucked up."

Act Four: Shame Endurance

Have you ever had people look at you with disgust or as though you're not even there? Have you ever had this happen in the same room as the cast and producers of *Argo*?

For the next two hours, Robert and I endured a marathon of shame. Technically it was two hours, but it felt like at least eight. I want to be clear that it wasn't the cast staring at us; they were too preoccupied talking to like ten people at once and looking glamorous. The real stares came from the other folks that decided that they were famous by association and would treat Robert and I, aka The Little People, like shit. They ignored us if we had the gall to make small talk and gave us repulsed looks whenever they got the chance. The waiters and servers just kind of pretended we weren't there and gave us a wide berth when they walked around with hors d'oeuvres. Robert and I ended up hanging out at one buffet table and then slowwwwwly making our way to the other one and then slowwwwwly back, pretending the two of us weren't quickly depleting the mini-cupcakes and brownie bonbons meant for a hundred people.

Slowly, I felt anger bubbling up inside me. Maybe it was the dirty looks, or probably the sugar from all the cupcakes. Why were they treating us like this? Why were we so ashamed and why were they looking us up and down, scoffing? Just because of clothes? And because we were eating the food that no one was touching? I, Ellie Guzman, was a due-paying SAG member who had been chosen for the committee, and I was just as entitled to be there as everyone else. Robert was my guest that I was told to bring and he deserved to be there too! We weren't less than everyone else just because we were underdressed! Hell no! I was going to talk to Bryan Cranston, so help me God.

Act Five: My Apologies to Bryan Cranston

I dutifully marched myself over to Heisenberg himself, who was about halfway across the room and talking to just two other people. This was my chance. I butted myself into their little triangle, and he gave me a little nod, but I quickly looked down at the ground and realized I had lost all ability to move.

He was interviewing with some guy from Vanity Fair, and the other dude was mooching off of the interview for his own publication, and I just kind of stood there. I literally just stood there. I wouldn't be surprised to learn that there was drool coming out of my mouth. I stood there, transfixed, listening and waiting to get a word out but knowing that I would be too chicken to say anything. I ended up staring at Bryan Cranston for what was probably ten straight minutes without saying a word and then slowly slinking away once my legs regained feeling. Not a proud moment.

Act Six: Finally, The Movie

They opened the doors to the theater, and at this point Robert, for some horrifying reason, decided that he was going to eat *all of the remaining food on the buffet tables.* He started stuffing leftover food in his mouth and, compelled by hunger and shame and years of being told that you do NOT waste food, I too began rushing up and down the table and stuffing every goddamn tiny biscuit and little weird egg thing in my mouth. I like to think that "Bad Reputation" played in the background the whole time while I ran around consuming cake pops like I was in an eating contest.

Once Robert and I realized we were essentially the only two people left in the room, we made our way into the theater and got extremely shitty seats. It was fine, though, because by this point we honestly just wanted to go home. We watched the movie in a haze, digesting the treats and the trauma. After the movie there was a Q&A, and I don't remember a single thing from it. Half of it was the shame, half of it was the quiche coma.

The Q&A ended and everyone began filing out back through the ballroom hall. As we were leaving, I saw John Goodman walking toward us, and I blurted out the only thing I could think of to prove to myself that I could indeed talk to these people.

"I loved your work in *Community*, Mr. Goodman!"

John Goodman stopped in his tracks and gave me the saddest look any human being has ever given me in my life. He sighed heavily.

"Thanks, sweetheart."

Robert and I never spoke of the event again.

Broke Living Tip #11:

If you can't afford to have a pet, go to the dog park and stand outside, pressing your face against the fence and howling. You might end up with a new forever family.

Whitewashed

Growing up, I heard three kinds of statements from my extended Salvadoran family. They were either: 1) a negative comment on my appearance and/or weight, 2) a compliment on my grades which eventually led to a strained relationship with my cousins, or 3) something about me being "so white".

Weirdly enough, I felt uncomfortable about the first two but not so much about the third. As a kid, I knew being fat and a nerd were not desirable traits, but being called white wasn't the worst thing in the world.

I grew up hearing comment after comment from both family and strangers alike about how being white was the desirable thing to be. My parents would always say that I'd end up meeting a nice white boy in college and having half white babies. My sister was frequently complimented for her fair skin by like 90% of the Latino people we encountered in our daily lives at laundromats and grocery stores. When I asked my mom if I could go to a white kid's house party in high school, her usual strictness about my social life melted away and she barely took a breath before saying yes.

I wasn't taught to hate non-white people, but it was drilled into my head that the best thing for me to do for myself and my own success was to be as white as possible and shove down my Latina roots. I'm not outwardly white passing, but every time I talked about books or green juice I felt like the world saw me as whiter and whiter. Of course, that's stupid and doesn't mean anything, but the way my aunts and uncles sliced it, those were the activities of fancy white ladies. Girls like the Guzmans had babies and cooked for their husbands, and girls like the Guzmans' bosses did yoga and had college degrees. Not ready for babies or a husband, I found myself subconsciously leaning into the whole "you're so white" thing as a way to avoid what I saw as my Latina destiny. As a result, I suppressed my Central American roots. It was fucked up and wrong, but it was all that I knew at the time.

It took a long time for me to realize what I was doing to myself, which I am not proud of. In college, I'd frequently be invited to Latino student mixers and I wouldn't go, telling myself that I didn't need to segregate myself from white students. What I know now is that embracing my community in college would've gone a great way to make me feel less lonely because no matter how you slice it, humans are social animals, and it's nice to feel like you belong once in a while. But instead I locked myself in my dorm, trolled around on Tumblr, and watched *30 Rock* for the billionth time.

Weirdly enough, it was my time doing the supposedly "white" thing (according to my aunts) of getting an education that made me realize I was being a fucking idiot by letting myself be brainwashed this way. As a human biology major, I had to read a lot about anthropology. I was slowly learning how to think critically about culture and academia, and it was just a matter of time until it all clicked. Suddenly, it was like the proud Salvadoran that had been in me all along burst out, throwing pupusas into the air like Frisbees.

I reflected on how my upbringing had impacted my worldview, especially toward my racial and ethnic identity. What does it mean for me that I'm brown but have been told repeatedly that I "act white"? What do I do as a Salvadoran American who doesn't fit in with either culture? Why do I view certain things as "white"? What does that mean about the things I view as "brown"? How do I break this cycle of thinking, for myself and for my family? How am I just noticing this now?

I began speaking more Spanish. I let myself enjoy our music, playing it on speaker instead of my headphones. I read up on Salvadoran history, wanting to get to know my country better. I stopped listening when people called my neighborhood "ghetto" or "sketchy. I learned to love my dark wavy hair and olive-toned skin.

Then I looked inward at my own family and community. Why were other Latinos telling me that being white was a desired trait? What did they think of people that were darker than me? I realized for the first time in my life the scope of racism within my own minority community. I felt so ignorant for not realizing this all my life.

I had open and honest conversations with my African American and Afro-Latinx friends about anti-blackness in the Latino-Hispanic community and how pervasive it is. I hadn't even realized that Latin American countries also participated in the Atlantic slave trade, and that even though there are millions of Afro-Latinx people in our countries, we still think of light-skinned Latinos as the default. I'm ashamed that I was so ignorant about it but at the same time, it's important to talk about it in case it helps anyone else learn.

The desire to be white or telling others they "act white" comes from a place of racism, regardless of how unintentional it is. Being a minority is hard enough without buying into that kind of bullshit. This is unfortunately an age of xenophobia and racism, and now more than ever, we can't be doing this to each other. At the end of the day, no matter what, I know that I'm going to be labeled first and foremost as a Latina woman. That's what happens to people like me. We're referenced to as a "Latina writer" or a "Latino politician" or whatever rather than just the occupation itself. White is still the unspoken default; it's on us to change that.

Broke Living Tip #12:

Make your financial situation part of your social media brand. Now when you tell your friends you can't go out with them this weekend because you need to pay rent, it'll seem cutely on brand instead of a stone-cold bummer.

Budgeting

My favorite comment I've ever received on any piece of written work was from a gentleman who kindly let me know that money is not the key to happiness. I was truly shaken to my core by this revelation. *You're saying it's not? I can be happy AND poor???*

To be fair, money really isn't the key to happiness, but without money, I have a hard time seeing myself being happy. I grew up living paycheck to paycheck, and let me tell you, I would not recommend it. Things are better now, and every year of my life that passes, I become more and more financially stable. Weirdly enough, I'm starting to pile together some savings, which is something my parents could never do. I'm on time with my student loan payments. I can pay for pressed juice. I own more than one bra. It might not be much, but it feels like a fortune to me. And you know what? I'm way happier! Imagine that!

Money is not the answer to being happy, but it certainly does help. It relieves stressors, and I'll always take more if I'm offered it. My view toward money growing up was that I should try to collect as much as possible, and that was essentially it. Money was always this weird, abstract thing to me; when I didn't have it, I cared about it, and when I did have it, I didn't care about it. I didn't learn until recently that even when I do have it, I should still care about it. In fact, I should care even more, because I should be managing it.

It wasn't until I had enough money to throw around that I realized that I should have been budgeting this entire time. I always budgeted when resources were scarce, but once I hit a comfortable amount, I would neglect budgeting entirely. It finally clicked that this is a "me" problem, because I actually have more power than I give myself credit for. I'm just so used to being powerless that I didn't recognize that the ball is now in my court. That's my fault, I'll admit it.

I grew up thinking that saving money basically amounted to gathering drops in a bucket. My parents had a debt of several thousand dollars, so their logic was, "Hell, this $20 pizza isn't going to make a difference in our debt, so let's just get it and have a good time. This $30 manicure isn't going to help with our massive debt, so fuck it, let's feel good for a bit. This $50 isn't going to make a difference when Ellie goes to college, so let's just go watch a movie as a family and make good memories."

I absorbed this logic and didn't realize how deeply ingrained it was in me until I realized that when you add all of that up, it's $100, and it only takes ten of those to make $1000. Once I began applying math to my actual money, it sank in that I was burning it all. I was single-handedly throwing away my own peace of mind for no reason. It's one thing to be tired on a Monday and order a $20 delivery in dumplings. It's another thing to do that every few days and realize that you've spent close to $200 on delivered food in a month.

I recently began writing down everything I spend money on and, weirdly enough, it's very different than mindlessly scrolling through my banking app and shrugging when I see another $20 spent on cute stationary. Physically writing stuff down gives me the time to process that I, a grown woman, am spending what amounts to hundreds a month in overpriced coffee, overpriced juice, overpriced hamburgers, overpriced booze, and overpriced kawaii unnecessary shit. Like, really Ellie? You spent $40 on stickers in Little Tokyo? STICKERS?!

That's when I realized that, with my carelessness, I was repeating the Guzman money cycle all over again. I cringed so hard I think I tweaked my neck. It's one thing to think that you've turned into your parents when you try to haggle at the pharmacy or don't trust enabling location services on your phone. It's a whole other thing when you realize that you're a couple more bad decisions away from facing the same years of financial struggle and bankruptcy that they have.

My identity was also thrown for a complete loop. I have always been the poor kid in my environment, whether it be school, work, or just hanging out with friends. Now that I'm no longer an assistant and can afford to have my own place, am I no longer the actual poor kid? Am I just so shitty with money that it seems like I'm the poor kid? Oh God, if I budget, will it actually feel like I can live... *comfortably!?!??!*

So now I budget, and it feels fucking weird. It feels weird to tell myself I can only spend $40 on coffee a month. It's uncomfortable to think twice before I buy ten $3 face masks because yeah, $3 doesn't seem like much, but there's ten of them, and that's $30. It's a little sad to have home-cooked rice and chicken again when I know that with a click of a button I can order delivery. Then I think about my future, about my imaginary kids' futures, about taking care of my elderly parents down the road, and I realize that it's on me to break this cycle. I'm privileged enough now that I can make smart decisions with my money, and I refuse to screw my future self over.

Oh God, I'm actually kind of privileged now, aren't I?

I set aside about $100 a month to just do whatever I want. If I want to go watch a movie, get my nails done, or buy an inky pen, it comes out of that set amount. It's nice because I'm not mindlessly spending as much as I would have, but I'm still treating myself. It's also crazy to see how quickly $100 goes by. No wonder I had no savings before.

I'm the first person in my family to have a disposable income, and I'm also the first to budget with a surplus. Yes, it's small now, but it's a surplus nonetheless, and it feels weird, but I feel happy and at peace financially. Budgeting is not natural to me and I still slip up sometimes, but it's what I must do. I happen to be the first, but I most certainly do not want to be the last. I hope to help my younger sister become more empowered financially too. We'll climb out of this hole together, because for the first time, there's absolutely no reason for us to be living in it.

Broke Living Tip #13:

Your middle school best friend's recently divorced dad makes a decent sugar daddy in a pinch. Hypothetically speaking of course. Wink.

The New Normal

I'm a firm believer in chaos. To me, life is random and atoms are smashing and now we're here and someday we won't be. It's scary, but to be honest I like the possibility of the unknown.

Despite those feelings, I've always been a planner. I think it was my way to try to control my destiny in the randomness of the universe. I always knew life was extremely temporary and so I wanted to make as big of an impact as I could. I felt that medicine would be a good way to do that.

I majored in human biology in college and it was excruciatingly difficult. I graduated by the skin of my teeth. I think what made it so hard was that my heart was never fully in it; college was simply the means to an end that I had sort of convinced myself I wanted. I enjoyed the puzzle of medical diagnosis, but everything else about it was mind-numbing. Nevertheless, I worked in cancer research and racked up volunteer hours at an emergency room, debating my career path but loving the thrill of our team saving patients. Medical school became a respectable goal to work towards, and it beautifully outlined the rest of my life.

Even though I was focused on medicine, I could never shake my love for writing. Growing up, I spent hours every day dreaming up worlds for myself. In elementary school, I would watch people on the street from my window with little binoculars like Harriet the Spy, and I would make up stories for their lives. In middle school, I'd write short stories and then sit in front of my family's TV in the evenings, watching Jon Stewart and Stephen Colbert on Comedy Central and scribbling down my favorite jokes in my composition notebook so I could enjoy them later. In high school, I took full advantage of the internet and educated myself in all things comedy: the work of Amy Sedaris, *Monty Python*, *SNL*, anything Tina Fey touched, silly sketches on YouTube. In college, I did a little standup and kept writing whatever I could: short stories, sketches, topical one-liners for a fake late night show. Though I loved comedy and writing, I knew one thing for sure: it was a pipe dream. Medical school was clearly the obvious choice, so I kept my whims to myself.

Then *The Mindy Project* came out when I was 19, and I felt a lump in my throat watching the first episode. Here was a woman of color who had a creative vision and made her own show. She rose through the ranks writing and developed her own series. I didn't want to act, but I wanted to create, to write my own stuff. If she could do it, I could too, right? I was only a college sophomore; maybe I could change my major? I talked myself out of it, telling myself I wanted a stable future.

At 22 years old, I graduated college and naturally was jobless for six months. I started writing and posting blog pieces on the internet, purely silly shit like "10 Sexual Positions for Underachievers" and "Please Give Me This Horrible Soul-Sucking Job." I got a few thousand readers on Medium and had some pieces picked up by publications like *The Huffington Post*, but I knew the internet was fickle. I kept applying to jobs in medicine like being a nurse recruiter or a medical scribe so that I could get some experience before taking the medical school test and applying, happy that at least some people were reading my writing. It brought me a lot of joy to write to my heart's content, even as I delivered food all over LA because I was still unemployed.

In February 2016, I got the weirdest email out of the blue. It was the Story Editor from a show at a well-known animation studio, and he was writing to let me know that there was a Script Coordinator position open. He said he and his writing team had seen my writing online, and they wanted to see if I'd be interested in interviewing. I thought this was a lie, or phishing, or that he was going to kill me, but I didn't have too much to lose so I showed up. It wasn't until I was staring at a display full of Emmy's that I realized I was actually there.

I interviewed with him and his team and the whole time I had absolutely no idea what we were talking about. I was honestly just happy to be there. Animation is a complicated beast, and I was 100% not ready for the job. Regardless, I left with a smile on my face. I could not believe TV writers had read and enjoyed my writing, wow!

I got an email a few days later from HR saying I did not get the job, and I was honestly fine with it. It became a fun story with my friends: "Imagine if I got that?"

A month later I was offered a medical scribe position at an emergency room, and I took it. I did that for eight months and it was incredibly rewarding work. I wouldn't trade it for the world. My job was to take notes for the doctors, and I was present at all patient encounters, from prescription refills to the traumas. I worked crazy hours around the clock, and after taxes made about $9 an hour. The scribe job was part-time and had no benefits, other than a 10% discount at the cafeteria. The job was also 18 miles away from my place, so I think in terms of gas and paying for meals and new sets of scrubs, I might have lost money working there. It was exhausting work, and I almost quit after we lost not one but two little boys in a day. But the work was so gripping and life-changing that I felt compelled to stay. The doctors encouraged me and said I'd make a great doctor, and so I started planning to take classes at a community college to boost my chances of getting into medical school.

The job was unlike anything else, but it was also wearing me out financially and physically. I wondered if I would be willing to make the sacrifices necessary to be a successful medical student. I knew that I'd have to take on a tremendous amount of debt to be able to afford a medical education, and I'd have to give up my personal life for a few years. I also knew that none of that would stop me if I was 100% sure it was what I wanted. I kept hesitating and putting off taking classes, because I knew, deep down, that I didn't truly want it. I felt most at peace with myself when I was writing, editing, and connecting with an audience. There was nothing like it, but I felt incredibly selfish. Shouldn't I choose to help people with medicine? Won't being a doctor help me and my family more financially? Aren't creative jobs unstable?

In January 2017, I checked my email and felt my guts fall to the floor; the animation studio was reaching out again, nearly a year later, this time about interviewing for a Production Assistant position. It turned out that one of the writers from the previous show that I interviewed for now had his own show, and my resume had been passed along from last time. I felt a weird shift; suddenly I was more nervous than I'd ever been in my whole life. Something felt different.

I went to the interview and I thought it went well. I continued with my life, working at the ER and skimming community college catalogues. One day on my lunch break in the hospital cafeteria I got a phone call; it was the animation studio offering me the PA job! I jumped about five feet in the air and accepted on the spot. I wrote down the information on my little medical notepad, and I went back to work with my hands trembling and a completely inappropriate gigantic grin for the rest of the day.

I quit the ER and was able to take a break until April since I thankfully lived with my parents at the time. I spent the time writing as much as I could and delivering food to make a little extra money.

I started as a PA in April 2017, worked on one show and moved on to my second show in October 2018, and then became a Production Coordinator in December 2018. The learning curve in animation is very steep, and I was incredibly lucky to work with some wonderful and supportive teams.

In April 2019, I was promoted to Script Coordinator on a different show. I believe in chaos and I embrace it, but I will also say that everything happened exactly the way it needed to. I'm so glad to be at this company now, but I feel that my time at the ER absolutely needed to happen to make me the person I am today. I'm great at handling stress, at problem-solving on the fly, and at not batting an eyelash when anything weird happens. I also know now that I was not ready for the Script Coordinator job back in 2016. That would have been a disaster. Phew.

Best of all, I'm now taking concrete steps to actually make what I once thought was a pipe dream come true. I can actually be a writer in this new reality. As a matter of fact, I recently earned the opportunity to write an episode of the show that I'm the Script Coordinator for. It's currently a work in progress, and I'll be in shock about it for at least the next decade. I'm writing an episode of television. It's so crazy. I've been bursting into happy tears every chance I get. My heart is very full.

It's taken some time to adjust to my new normal over the past couple years and get in tune with what it is that I really want. I definitely felt guilty about leaving the career that I studied for behind. Thankfully, my parents responded to me ditching a medical career surprisingly well. They said all they care about is that I'm able to provide for myself, which is a huge weight off my shoulders. That could have gone another way completely.

The financial change has also been crazy. It says a lot about the healthcare system that I have better pay and benefits working on a cartoon than I did when I was watching people die on the regular. I know that the entertainment industry is more unstable than healthcare, but I feel that the pay and lack of medical school debt has balanced things out for me. For example, after my Script Coordinator promotion I was able to finally move out of my parents' place. It was a hard transition; throw pillows are expensive, but I feel more financially empowered than ever. It feels good to have my own space. I've shared a room with someone my entire adult life; I can finally fart in peace. I'm also very fortunate that my family is in the same city, so if it all goes sideways I have somewhere to lay my head.

Of course, I have to acknowledge that even in this new environment that I love so much, I'm still an outsider. TV writing is insanely male-dominated and white-dominated.

As a coordinator, I'm also still the poorest person in the room, but that would have also been the case as a doctor. Just how there's a wealth gap between assistants and producers, there's a gap between medical residents and attending physicians. The major difference is that it doesn't affect me as much as it used to when I was younger. Seeing women like Tanya Saracho, Mindy Kaling, Shonda Rhimes, Tina Fey, and others do it fills me with a weird high; I think the feeling is called "empowerment."

One thing this career change has taught me is that anything can happen. Who knows what chaos will ensue the next week, next month, or next year? Honestly, I'm pretty thrilled to find out.

Broke Living Tip #14:

Instead of paying for a professional (i.e. expensive) therapist who can help you deal with years of trauma, drink a bunch of Four Lokos and start a blog.

Twenty Six

My father was 26 in the late 1980s. He had been in the United States for about 9 years. He was a bachelor with a small apartment, and he spent his days hustling in any way he could; he worked as a driver, a window installer, a security guard, you name it. He made a few friends and was taken under the wing of a local repairman, but he had no family out here. He bettered his English by listening to The Beatles and Elvis Presley and used his skills to survive in Los Angeles.

My dad came to the US as a teenager. He fled El Salvador right near the beginning of the Salvadoran Civil War, a violent conflict that spanned from 1980 to 1992. As a young man, he was in danger of being forced to fight for either side. Thankfully he had an aunt that had the resources to get him to the US, and so he took the opportunity. Some of his friends weren't so lucky.

My mother turned 26 at the turn of the century. She's younger than my father, and they both came to the United States as teenagers in different decades. When my mom was 26, I was already seven-years-old and my sister was two-years-old.

For the vast majority of my mother's childhood, El Salvador was engaged in the Civil War. Her family sheltered her as much as possible, but there was always fear of kidnappings, death squads, and the other horrible realities of that war. Her own mother desperately wanted to give her a better life, and she'd heard good things about the United States from other family members who had made the trek and were now able to send back money. My mom was sent on her way to the US by herself, a tiny petite 17-year-old fending for herself.

But she made it, and she was able to live at her aunt's house and at least have the comfort of family while she adjusted to her new life. In her mid-twenties, my mother was making serious efforts to assimilate in the United States, taking classes at a local community college in English and Child Development while I was at school and my sister was at the free Head Start Daycare. She had spent ages 19-26 mostly taking care of her kids, cooking, and cleaning houses, and when the opportunity for more schooling came along, she jumped at it. Her evenings were spent doing homework, making dinner, and prepping us for the next day.

I turned 26 in April 2019. I have no kids or dependents, but I do have a cactus plant that is on the brink of death. In all seriousness, I'm grateful for my parents' sacrifices, because they've allowed me to live the relatively comfortable life that I have today. I know that's obvious for any first-generation family, but it's hard to fathom the gravity of it sometimes. When I look at my parents' experiences when they were my age versus mine now, I don't know if I could survive if I were in their shoes. I complain enough when the printer at work jams; I can't imagine being in a whole new country learning a whole new language as your old home is ravaged by war.

Of course, I've had my own struggles, and while they pale in comparison to what my parents went through, mine are still legitimate. I think because I've struggled, I can appreciate their sacrifices more. There have been moments in my life where I've had to summon the drive to keep going, even when I'm completely burned out and questioning what I'm even supposed to be doing with myself. It's during those moments that I realize I got that drive from my parents.

It took a long time, but I'm proud of who I am. I'm proud of being first generation Salvadoran American, of being a five foot tall Latina woman with hair that turns into a tumbleweed when it's humid out. I'm proud of my parents even when they're crazy, and I'm proud of my sister even when she's better than me. I'm proud that I grew up with knockoff Barbies and that I only had one pair of shoes at a time and that I've done crazy jobs like child acting and drinking sugar water for science.

I used to think that growing up struggling with money was a setback, but now I know that it's given me my strength. I thought my personality would change when I had a bit more money, but I've doubled down on my roots more than ever. It doesn't matter how much money I have or don't have, where I live, or what I wear.

No matter what, I'm proud of my rags.

About Atmosphere Press

Atmosphere Press is an independent, full-service publisher for excellent books in all genres and for all audiences. Learn more about what we do at atmospherepress.com.

We encourage you to check out some of Atmosphere's latest fiction and nonfiction releases, which are available at Amazon.com and via order from your local bookstore:

On a Lark, a novel by Sandra Fox Murphy
Ivory Tower, a novel by Grant Matthew Jenkins
Tailgater, short stories by Graham Guest
Plastic Jesus, short stories by Judith Ets-Hokin
The Quintessents, a novel by Clem Fiorentino
The Devil's in the Details, short stories by VA Christie
Heat in the Vegas Night, nonfiction by Jerry Reedy
Chimera in New Orleans, a novel by Lauren Savoie
The Neurosis of George Fairbanks, a novel by Jonathan Kumar
Blue Screen, a novel by Jim van de Erve
Evelio's Garden, nonfiction by Sandra Shaw Homer
Difficulty Swallowing, essays by Kym Cunningham
Come Kill Me!, short stories by Mackinley Greenlaw
The Unexpected Aneurysm of the Potato Blossom Queen, short stories by Garrett Socol
Gathered, a novel by Kurt Hansen
Unorthodoxy, a novel by Joshua A.H. Harris
The Clockwork Witch, a novel by McKenzie P. Odom
The Hole in the World, a novel by Brandann Hill-Mann
Frank, a novel by Gina DeNicola

About the Author

Ellie Guzman is a freelance writer and script coordinator working in animation television. She studied Human Biology at USC and jumps at any opportunity to bring it up. She enjoys saying she's going to the gym but not actually going, putting things in her shopping cart but never purchasing them, and eating salad purely out of the desire to say, "I ate a salad." She lives in Los Angeles, so please help her pay rent.